Paula +
I hope these
Ocean refresh
your soul!
Aifa
2020

THE
SALT
IN HIS
KISS

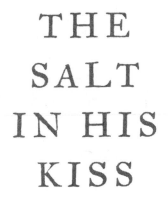

THE
SALT
IN HIS
KISS

ALFA

Bestselling author of
I Find You in the Darkness

CASTLE POINT BOOKS

This book is dedicated to those who find
themselves seeking solace in the sea when
memories threaten to take over.

*"Everyone becomes a poet when
their heart is screaming."*

A l f a

Introduction

You might have the soul of a mermaid if you find yourself inexplicably drawn to the ocean. For as long as I can remember, I've felt pulled by the salt, the sand, and the sea. I am lured by the ocean's promise of rejuvenation and relaxation. I scour the shores for one-of-a-kind treasures, and I spend countless hours in deep thought, meditation, and prayer. I release my worries and empty my troubled heart—*and the water never turns me away*. It is my hope that this book calls to the mermaid in you, and lets you know that you are never alone in matters of heartache and pain.

CONTENTS

BEACHCOMBING

MERMAID

My soul reminds me
that *I am* a mermaid.
A woman who longs to be held by the sea.

WALKING UPRIGHT

I learned to walk upright
with my head held high
whenever the *current*
tried to hold me under.

SCALES

I hide them under layers of self-doubt. The
remnants of yesterday are tattooed on my
skin in shimmery iridescent hues.
Memories of *what created me* itch, and a life
I hope never to *return to* breathes against
my windblown locks. These scales are a part
of me, but I do not share them with the
world. They are a reminder that I have swum
in the deepest parts of fathomless souls and
unearthed treasure troves *that I should
never have touched.*
Once you touch gold, your fingers *will
always burn* with a desire to have more.

THE SALT IN HIS KISS

Waves lick the horizon like
tongues tasting saltwater taffy.
Memories are always evoked by the division
of day and night, like tangerine sunsets on
late August nights and lips that taste like
freshly churned sorbet and the hint of an
afternoon swim.
I devoured every detail, every lie.
The memory of him is fading tonight, like
the sun sinking into the blanket of waves.
But I know it will return another day.
Another day spent remembering
the salt in his kiss.

LOVE

You are right.
We are different.
You have legs that can
walk away
from love,
and *I am a mermaid*
who is only capable
of swimming
in its depths.

BEACON

I see him shining in the distance:
Barrel chested, light emerging behind
fog as thick as leather and a book
of yesterdays.
His feet are grafted in rock
and cliffs guard his shoreline.
He *waits for me* to make the first move
because he wants to be my beacon,
but he will never succeed in *steering
my future.*

ADVICE

And when I held the seashell
up to my ear
and coaxed its advice,
it told me to quit lying
among the wreckage,
and to *begin again*.

SING

Your voice has always been so small, and you
have kept it silent because you did not
think your tale mattered.
You ground teeth and bit your lip in two to
hold in what you needed to share.
You're a grown woman now,
And, oh, how you've grown!
You *are* powerful even when you tremble.
So *sing*, sweet nymph. *Sing*.

TIDE

I would rather spend my restless days
watching the tide wash in and out
than drown in memories void of you.

ECLIPSE

And in the fragmented darkness,
I knew that his lunar smile
would captivate the moon
and always be the reason
for my soul's eclipse.

WINDBLOWN

The ocean is the only thing
that keeps me sane.
It accepts me just as I am.
Windblown.

SUMMARY

The waves are rhythmic,
just like his breathing.
How many nights did I
watch his chest rise and fall.
In and out—
a summary of our love.

FEAR

In retrospect, I never walked right.
I was dragged behind those I allowed to lead
the way.
I was distrusting of my own footing,
terrified of standing front and center, so I
let them guide the way. I was a straggler
along on their journey, helping them fulfill
the passions they pursued. Making myself
believe that I was quiet and shy.
That's the thing about fear. It keeps you
prisoner by counting on your silence
and compliance.
The only way to overcome it is to meet the
darkness head on. Once you've conquered the
unknown, it will never have control over
you again.

SEA SPRITE

He would leave
as so many before him
had done.
They never understood
her intensity
or her transparency.
They walked around in masks,
being what the world
wanted them to be
while she chose to live
authentically.
A sea sprite
who has trouble
walking on dry land.

BECAUSE OF HIM

Even if you want him to know you are lost
without him, force yourself to wipe the
agony and tears from your face *if you
see him.*
He will not run to you and say, "Sweetheart,
why does your head hang so low?"
But *he will notice* if your smile **is not**
because of him.
A mermaid's tears are sacred,
and are not to be given
to those who have walked away.

SUNSET

Every evening as I
store my hues
for another day,
I wonder:
Will they find me
if I hide behind
the sunset?

BALMY

The air is biting
from the sting
of his storm.
But my heart
is balmy
from the self-love
I keep soaking in.

MOTIVATION

They told me I could never be what my heart
wanted me to be.
How ironic that their words
were the motivation I needed
to prove them all wrong.

TALES

As long as the tales you weave
are authentic
and spun
with yarns of truth,
you will bestow generations
after you
with sentimental lore
of a passionate life
well lived.

HOME

She wears a seashell
close to her heart
so she can hear
the sound of home.

VANITY

For so long I thought it
a sin of vanity
to love myself.
And if truth be told,
I still feel a little squeamish
in my own skin.
But being uncomfortable
just reminds me
that self-love needs to be
reinforced daily,
until I wear it just like
my favorite pair of jeans.

LEAN ON ME

Lean on me.
I need to feel strong
and unfailing
for someone.
This is how I gauge
my worthiness
on the days
I feel most unworthy.

BEING THERE

I have realized that I make up
for *not being there for myself*
by always being there for others.

OPEN SPACES

How many walls
have you torn down
trying to give your heart
the open spaces
it craves?

ACCOUNTABLE

Hold *yourself* accountable.
Your happiness is not optional,
and is in no one else's hands
but your own.

WILLING

Are you willing to take the chance at
achieving your dreams?
What is it that you feel stirring inside when
you are tucked between the calm of day and
night? Your mind must wander, and your
heart must hold your hand and travel
somewhere important—where do you go?
Wherever you visit is where the treasure in
your oyster heart resides.
Pearls of passion are hidden there, and I
dare you to pry it open and peek inside.

CLOUDS

The clouds encroach. I watch them march
overhead like invaders: Menacing and
threatening with their heaviness.
They are mesmerizing in their raw display.
I feel their impact and their fury. They are
most often revered for their appearance
against blue, dappled skies...
but we need to remember that clouds get
angry, too.
Nothing is immune from passion.

WHERE ARE YOU?

I raise my hands up,
straining the muscles
of my heart.
Pleading with the moon
to shine down on you
and pinpoint where you
are beneath its shadow of
nothingness.

REFLECTION

Are you ever going to look away from the
mirror and see the eyes that already hold
you in their reflection?
The mirror you clutch so closely does not
define you, unless you allow it to. It does
not have arms to hold you. It will never
respond with the true love you desire.
Your life will not hold value if you seek it
from magic glass that you have to hold just
right to gain satisfaction.
Will you ever be capable of loving another
soul the way you ache to love your own?

RUNAWAY

I have run away
my entire life.
I have run so love
can never catch me.
But can you
really outrun true love?

LAVA

I am forever a woman
who stores emotions
and hoards memories.
A mermaid displaced
inside a volcano.
Trying to swim
through the lava
without getting burned.

MORNING BREATHS

The morning breathes upon
my flesh like
whispered promises and bad decisions,
like harsh, heated exhales while traipsing
through another humid day.
I'm bent and curved.
But when my feet touch the sand,
and my nose inhales the ocean's tonic,
my spirit rises
and my spine straightens,
and I walk into acceptance.

GALE

Are you ever going to chase after the wind
that knocked you off your feet years ago? Or
are you going to *let it think* it got the best
of you?
You would be amazed at what you can contain
if you stand still and absorb its strength.
Get knocked down and then stand another
day. Back and forth until you have a
rubber resolve.
Eventually your legs will become so strong
that a gale will sail on by and you won't
feel the air move.

I BELIEVE

I believe in magic and folklore.
Ancestral stories passed down through
centuries on voyages aboard ships that have
planted me where I am today. I believe in
storms that blow humanity across the
landscape of the earth like speckled
stardust, scattering souls where they are
meant to thrive. I believe in destiny and
second chances, and that the Universe
always has the last word. And I will always
believe that at any given moment, a message
in a bottle may land at my feet and bring my
true love a step closer.

ROYAL

In all the fairytales I've ever read, the
woman has to prove herself of worth to a
man of royal blood.
And here I am,
just trying to find the one who is worthy of
my royal heart.

CONTROL

Galaxies are contained within my chest.
I'm grateful to have kept the parts of me
that I once threw into bays and waterways
in hopes of attracting a sailor.
I thought that by putting myself in their
path that I could navigate their soul and
mine to connect. But it doesn't work
that way.
You can't go looking for love. *Love
is all powerful.*
It is in control. It will find you.

POWER

"And you had the power...
an eloquent way of touching
celestial bodies with your words
and
    making
         stars
            sing."

SOMEWHERE ELSE

I encounter myriad people every day.
Walking past me but seldom looking up.
I wonder if they are too afraid to make eye
contact for fear someone might see the
despair they hold.
I *cannot be* the only one walking around
wishing I was somewhere else.

MERMAID MONEY

Why has this earth turned its back on me
when I have given it my all? I watch youth
fade and it gives me age in its place.
I gave my hours and it gave me dollars that
bought me material things that in no way
brought me comfort.
I've offered my heart and it returned it
in stone.
But I still carry my purse of sand dollars
close to my heart. My dowry from the sea.
Hoping that I can use it one day
to give *to the one meant for me.*

TWISTER

And just like that
he blows you over.
You put your hand flat
against the wall
when he walks in
the room.
Anything to make the air
stop spinning.
You've heard of a force of nature before.
But you've never been leveled by a twister
in your heart...
before him.

CLOSING TIME

Never fall for the man who waits til
closing time
 to take you home.
The man you want
would rather be taking you out,
not just taking you in.

PLUNGE

You cannot
let another person
love you
only
physically.
Their love
needs to
swim in your
depths
and tangle in
your hair.

BEACH FACE

My mind repeats the discontent my
heart endures.
And yet I press the lips you once loved into
a forced smile... *and I carry on.*
There are days I show my strength by
opening an eye to see if it's light or
dark out.
And I carry on.

WISHING WELL

My body is a wishing well.
Look closely at your reflection.
You come to visit at times,
oblivious to the fact
that I've granted every
wish you've carelessly
tossed away.

RISING

He lifted me up,
held me in arms
of hope
and determination,
and carried me
from the past
into the present.

SAPPHIRES

Because of my past I am hesitant to look
closely at eyes. I used to love sapphires and
how they reminded me of the sky and
airplanes, and drinks on beaches,
suntanning, and gazing into trust I thought
would last forever.
I used to enjoy looking into eyes before he
held me close and made me look into his as
he was telling me he was leaving, *and that
he wanted one last look in mine before
he did.*

SHIPWRECKED

I've seen them wash ashore.
Shipwrecked souls who lost their way.
Vessels navigating by moonlight
instead of the sun's revealing rays.
I've seen them wash ashore.
Stunned and numb.
Needing rescuing.
Just like me.

REJUVENATION

I make my way here
to avoid the breakdown.
To explore my thoughts.
My bones are supple
among the waves,
and my worries
are brittle
as I cast them
into the sea.

BLINDFOLDED

You can sail the world over and not
encounter the same love twice in
this lifetime.
Every soul is layers deep,
and we are not meant to explore all.
But with fate you will encounter the one
who blends the colors of the
world flawlessly.
And from that day forward you could
pick him out of a crowd blindfolded.
Because when you're in love, your heart sees
things your eyes cannot fathom.

FOOTSTEPS

Why is it
that goodbyes
never stick
the way
the echoes
of footsteps
do?

SALT

I look out at the white sands that resemble
salt, and they remind me of everything
perfect in the world.
Salted caramel.
The salt I taste in the sea.
The salt in a perfect rebuttal.
The memory of tasting the salt of his lips
after an ocean swim.

BITE

The lure of the sea
dangles as bait
and even though
I will never trust
my sea legs,
I remind myself
that my mind is sharp
and my *bite* is hard.

HUNGRY

I inhale salt
and foam,
filling my lungs
with the sea.
I come to the place
that consumed you.
All of our yesterdays
well in my eyes
and mix with the waves
of regret in my throat,
and I force myself
to taste your memory,
and I swallow
hungrily.

RIPTIDE

The riptide wrenched you away,
gathering your promises,
depositing them
on foreign shores
like whitecaps
on a Friday night
beer mug.

WANDERERS

Do you trust the ones who are always
searching, always packing for the
next adventure?
They want you to understand
that wanderlust feeds them.
But they never ask you to experience
it with them.
They expect you to be standing there at the
dock, hair billowing in a welcome-home
breeze, holding a handmade sign held high.
You are a welcome mat when they wash
ashore, when they feel nostalgic and
need rest.
But their home is not with you.
It's out there among the waves they ride.
The ones that promise them freedom.

SEA STACKS

MUZZLE

They talk down to her because of her beauty.
Like her face has no need of a tongue.
They listen to the sounds her hips make as
she sashays into the room.
She is used to her looks being a muzzle
to her voice.
Because they only hear what they want
to hear.

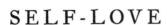

SELF-LOVE

She swam past
the self-doubt
and reached shores
of self-love.
And after that,
she always rescued
herself.

LIGHTHOUSE

You're looking to that
lighthouse for direction,
but you need to flip the switch,
and turn on the light
hidden along the
corridors of your soul.

HONEYSUCKLE

I am stagnant dreams
among winding honeysuckle
overtaking fences
surrounding townships
I have never visited,
lands I have never ventured to find.
I've spent wasted days in the deep end,
and it's high time
I came up for air.

WEAK LOVE

You think the distance between those in
love defines its depth or determines
its demise?
No...it's not about the distance.
People use distance as an excuse.
They want Easy-Bake Oven. Put it in
and take it out.
If it is true love, the distance evaporates.
Souls are magnetic and pull toward each
other. True love connects and latches
on forever.
Distance can be overcome; weak love cannot.

BLANKETS

I will meet you at the place where you
find comfort.
In the blanket of your sorrows.
In the pillows of your softness.
Acceptance will come from a heart that
soothes the weary and offers warmth to
those wandering in the cold.

PROTECTOR

If you let me
kiss the raindrops
away,
I promise to protect you
from the next
storm.

MOONLIGHT

You move with
spirit and grace,
and the stars
bow down
as you bask
beneath the
moonlight.
And shadows
have never felt
less menacing.

SLIP AWAY

Even after all this time, it is never you
whom I have regretted.
It was my inability to hold onto you as
the waves crashed against the place our
hearts called home.
There are those who run when the skies
grow grey and the wind roars, and then
there are others who choose to ride out
the storm.
My regret will always be that I let
you slip away instead of holding on with
all my might.

MIRAGE

I blinked, and the moment was gone.
Just like the last time with him.
How long does it take before your eyes are
able to remain level when locking gazes and
telling someone what you really want?
Was it all a mirage?
An illusion?
I still see him everywhere.
But surely the other half of my spirit is out
there searching for me, too.

HIDING

The rhythmic ripples can play tricks on you
at night. Shadows become company.
They play poker with your ghosts.
The moon winks because he knows his role is
only to highlight, but never to reveal.
You hide things in the quiet.
You hide the very things that need light in
your soul.

FORMATIONS

I have waterfalls
ambling down
formations
erected by
nature
and
men.

HOLIDAY

I create a Christmas tree
out of conches and pebbles
embedded in the sand
and place a starfish on top.
My tears rise with the upcoming tide.
I celebrate my holiday on the shore where
I am most thankful.
I'm celebrating the person
who swam her way
to the surface.

UNINHABITED

I leap.
I turn 360s at your command.
I surf on vibrations of your approval and
your denial.
I've lost myself somewhere.
My spine lives on an island uninhabited by
self-love or the strength to be found.
And this is just another day
until the ocean calls me home.

ANOTHER GIFT

The magic will return and find you in
the exact
spot you stopped believing.
It will seek you out,
and your chest will split wide open and
make room for a second chance.
Another gift that you never saw coming.
And maybe you will choose to believe again.

RUNNING

Is it any wonder
that my legs run away
from man and land
toward the place
where the sand
kisses its lover?

WISHES

I watch them rise out of the
surrounding loam.
One after the other, lighting up the
eastern sky.
Every wish upon a star that sank into
the ocean.
Absorbed by the sky.
Expelled from the sea.
And I wonder if our wishes are swimming
at the bottom of the ocean, too.

REACHING

I am reaching for something.
Something I cannot explain.
My spirit twists and turns,
the goal just beyond its grasp.
Something that is not here,
but exists somewhere.
I am reaching for something
beyond what I can see.
I am folding my hopes like paper airplanes,
and praying they find their way.
I am reaching, and I grasp nothing.

ADMISSIONS

I spend daylight
with a chest full
of nighttime admissions.
And I spend nighttime
praying that daylight
finds you beside me.

ABANDONED

My past washes upon the shore
with the sunrise.
And I regret never looking up at the
peach hues.
I've always kept my stare fixed on the
disarray; the discarded bits of me and you
that lie like abandoned wreckage for all the
beachcombers to sift through.
I step in footprints shaped like yours,
but they never fit the same way.
The dolphins and the birds ask about you,
and I tell them you'll be back another day.

HEAVY LOAD

How is it
I manage
to carry
yesterday
on my back,
and
tomorrow
on my knees?

UNDERSTANDING

Lapis skies
always bring
blue memories
of you.
And maybe
I come
to the ocean
because it
understands
my need
to remember
you.

STOIC

I see water as far as I can see.
Nothingness is everything.
It brims with more life than I will ever see.
And I realize that a person can die
from standing stoic on shore.
You don't have to *go into the water* to drown.

COLLECTOR

My fingers are gritty
from picking up treasures
I find hidden beneath my feet.
I comb the shore for collectibles,
easily discarded things
to hang on my inspirational wall.
Driftwood because nothing deserves to
travel alone.
Bark to remind me that seasons
encourage shedding.
Ropes that hold hearts prisoner.
Plastic because that's how you feel when you
live an inauthentic life.
Shells that echo the sounds of home.

EXITS

I still remember his exit.
Choppy,
like the water
that lapped
at my *faltering feet*
during my morning walk.

BEFORE AND AFTER HIM

Love comes from souls who listen to the songs in your heart, even if they are not in tune with it.

Love comes from self-acceptance and the realization that *you are more than worth* loving.

Love comes from the ocean and its stability. How it never leaves you and remains dependable day after day. It's always there to remind you that faith reigns and hope is but a ripple away.

Love comes from hearts who come unexpectantly into our lives and mark us so indelibly that we define ourselves from that point on: *before and after him.*

MAIDEN

I am lyrical.
I sing the words I write.
Tunes of heartache
and harmony of pain.
I sing sad songs
as I sit on a sandy shore
that plays backup singer.
And the ocean
always upstages me.

EXPLORE

You always
have to explore
a shipwreck
to find where the
treasure is hidden.

PROMISES

Will you promise
to hold her head
above the water
on the days
she sinks too deep?

AUDIBLE LOVE

He used to bring me flowers until he swam
through my soul.
Now he gifts me with seashells, so his love
is always heard.

THE MAN TO MY MAID

I wonder if he will be my forever sunset.
My unexpected sunrise.
My treasure washed ashore.
Sand between my thighs.
The shells that I collect.
The wind that fondles my hair.
Driftwood that stays put.
The *man* to my *maid*.

SEAWEED SOLACE

We should all hold kelp or seaweed in our
hands at least once *and feel its weight.*
Somehow it was torn free, forced from its
environment to wash ashore.
And I realize it doesn't belong here.
It's dying beneath the sun's rays.
It hurts. And *I know how it feels.*

DESPERATION

The seagulls look at me with wise eyes.
*They know hunger and desperation when
they see it.*

CASTING

I bring my worries
and my troubles
to the cliffs
and exhale them.
They are carried away
and dispersed at sea.
Giving them the proper
seafaring burial
they deserve.

KAHUNA

He was a heartache
with a heartbeat
tuned to the beach.
He swam in
with the tide,
and always closed
his exit
riding high
on the waves.

FALLING OFF THE WAGON

I keep my mind clear
and my heart detoxed.
I will not let myself
get intoxicated
by the likes of you
again.
Falling off the wagon
never feels good.

SPIRITS

The breezes blow across the sand and with
them come the sounds of clinking. I hear
glasses chime and turn to watch a couple
celebrate their time together—*the same way
we used to.*
I don't handle spirits well anymore.
Not the kind consumed from celebratory
glasses, nor the kind that clank around in
the corners of my heart.

CONSUME

If you are going to love her
you better be able to consume
all of her
the same way the ocean does.

CONDUIT

Be a conduit for kindness and compassion.
Be a lightning rod
so that even when buried
in the sand,
you create works of art
from the storms
that *dare* to pass over you.

STORM SURGE

When I stare entranced
at the energy
of an oncoming storm
rolling across the water,
the skies and their weight
of gloominess
make the storm's persistence
no less lovely.

EROSION

There was a time.
Before the sea.
Before I discovered me.
I was dead in a way
that lies numb.
When winter boots were stomping
upon my decaying layers,
I didn't even
flinch.

NEVER GIVE UP

I sit snug in the sand,
my fears burrowed into its forgiving weight.
I watch the ocean lap at my feet,
and with each tickle I count breaths.
I let its power fill my lungs
and I exhale with renewed purpose.
Because if it *never gives up,*
why should I?

ACCOMMODATING

I walk past homes
with lights glowing inside,
and well-worn welcome mats
inviting outside.
And my soul longs to be
just as accommodating.

LETTING GO

I watch the lights rumba in the bonfire.
Plumes of smoke resemble *purposely*
burned intentions.
The flames crawl upward until the sky
catches them open-fisted, bequeathing them
to the Universe and snatching them from
my life.
And just like that, when you really want to
let something go, you have an *authentic
send off.*
And you begin to heal.

SEA GLASS

I am lost in turquoise currents.
Billowing whitecaps beckon
me to take a sip of *life*.
They are convincing in coaxing me
to quench my thirst
with *all the little things*
I have denied myself while
building my impenetrable walls.
I'm not as strong as I look.
You may see rock walls,
but those are iridescent sea glass pieces
bordering my war-ravaged shores.

BACKWARDS

I never know what time it is.
Time and I broke it off when
it couldn't stop moving forward,
leaving me somewhere in the past.
When you spend your hours
trying to live in a time that is gone,
a clock is not your champion.

BREATHING HIM IN

Imagine inhaling
the feeling of
Christmas,
and exhaling forever.
That's what breathing him in
felt like.

HOOK, LINE, AND SINKER

I will tell you what saved me from the hook
of his fishing line. *I played hide and seek.*
Every time he cast, and sat patiently, I
would tug a bit *and then float away.* Maybe
the insecure parts of me wanted to see how
long he would sit on the banks before going
home empty handed.
My friends told me I was lucky I never
got caught.
*But I regret to this day not putting his
hook through my soul.*

THALASSIC ROWING

I don't blame him for sailing away and
embarking on a journey that chased
the stars.
I knew he loved the sea as much as he
loved me.
But if he had asked, I would have helped him
row *endlessly*.
I would have quieted the waters to a lull and
helped him navigate *forever*.

STARGAZER

I wonder if you saw that star
that just flickered.
We used to count the stars that blinked,
thinking they were winking at us. We
thought they could hear our conversations,
that they somehow picked and chose who to
grant wishes to. So we would act the fools,
and boldly talk to the sky and tell the
stars about our hopes and dreams.
And now every time I see a star, and see it
winking at me, I wonder if it is telling me
to be patient. Maybe, just maybe, you're
wishing for me, too.

MISS ME

The Human says:
I'll do whatever it takes
to ensure that you miss me.
The Mermaid says:
There are other fish in the sea
to save and *to destroy*.

SHARKS

I've visited the mountains,
but lions live there.
It seems
I'm more attracted
to sharks.

ALWAYS EMPTY

I am banter on quiet breaths.
Restricted on a swollen night.
Arms that hold nothing,
yet grasp at the air.
I am bottled promises
and empty oaths.
I am railroad tracks
leading to nowhere.
I am everything,
but feel like I'm nothing.

THALASSOPHILE

The ocean and I have the best of
conversations. It sweeps me off my feet
and soothes my edges *while saying nothing
at all.*

ERUPTION

He is amused by you.
He has never seen a volcano trapped *within
a goddess.*
But don't worry.
His laughter will fade when he sees your
self-worth erupt.

LONGEST BREATH

I take in the longest breath of my life
knowing that if I become lost,
I will never be found.
But that is the purpose of this excursion:
to discover what it is *I am missing.*

PAUSES

I've paused when I should have said yes.
And I've paused when I should have said no.
And still, I find you
in the pause between every breath.

DREDGING

WATERS

I will entice you
to dive into waters
you have avoided.
Not the deep seas
where you hide,
but the waters
surrounding my shore.
The waters surrounding
home.

LEGENDARY

I am not a wishful delusion conjured by men
who've been at sea too long.
I'm not an apparition that materializes to
entice you after having sipped rum from the
bottom of a barrel. Maybe my elusiveness is
my draw, my lair of mystique.
It's true. I am legendary. They offer prize
money to prove my existence, and yet you
know me intimately, and still you
are frightened.
Your seafaring heart justifies *its* fear by
following the call of the unknown.
You leave, rather than stay, because you are
afraid that fairytales come true.

DREDGING

It's at the bottom
And you are going to have
to heave and ho
and dig and throw
until you unearth
the layer that has never
been touched.
Excavate and sift.
Rub the grains
between your hands.
Feel the featherlight softness.
You're left with
Mermaid dust.

HEARTS TEAR

I wonder if the sounds
of hearts tearing
find you in the twilight
as the moon and the sun
say their goodbyes.

INJURY

Love is the bruise
that likes to remind you
of the injury
that has lasted
much too long.

STARFISH

If I stand just so
under the sunset
as it captures
the ocean waves,
my hair turns as green
as my eyes,
and the starfish
mistake me for a
mermaid.

COCKTAIL

She moved like a cocktail
of riptide
and rainbows,
and after you
felt her kick in,
you wanted
a double.

THEY MISJUDGE ME

I sit on the rocks and bask in the sunshine,
and I hear, "Are you trying to lure a man
to his death?"
So many have misjudged me.
They don't understand.
I am not here to lure humans
into the sea.
I am trying to escape humanity.

RHYTHM

I sometimes wonder if heartbeats control
their rhythm to synchronize with the ones
they love. Maybe when they slow, they are
enjoying the moment and waiting for the
other to pick up speed.
Maybe when they race, they are enticing
their beloved to run wild with them. To let
go and let the undercurrent pulse with
passion and show them worlds of
forgotten treasure.
And maybe when they stall and murmur it is
because they are catching their breath,
pausing because they are enamored with the
one they love, and no words will
ever suffice.

SOUL STROLL

I had to learn to let my soul stroll. I took
slow walks under dancing fireworks at dusk.
I reminded myself to look up, absorb, and
breathe, and not worry if my feet were
perfectly planted on the ground.
Sometimes you have to have faith that your
feet and your soul will find their own way.

RAVENS GASP

I've seen my share of ravens.
They follow me around,
waiting on me to give up.
Sometimes I stumble
just to watch
their hungry
little hearts
gasp.

HEIRLOOMS

She was the girl who grew up and refused to
let the fairytale of true love leave
her heart.
She combed the beaches in dawn's early light
looking for proof that a landscape can
change overnight.
That miracles wash ashore looking for
new homes.
She was the girl who still believed that
things washed away should be given another
chance, should be treasured and viewed
as heirlooms.

COASTAL GRACE

He was coastal grace in my storm,
and he brought peace to a mermaid
who lived her life *out of the water*.

OVER AND OVER AGAIN

The ocean holds the answers to all of the
questions the land can never answer.
I ride the waves and feel the power of
something beyond my control.
Consistency.
The ripples of the water pool at the sand's
curves and they gently kiss her *over
and over.*
Always coming back.
The sand doesn't change. It stays true to
itself, and the ocean *still comes back.*
And kisses her *over and over again.*

SOUNDS

When you carry the sound
of the ocean in your heart,
you are never alone
because your soul
is never quiet.

WITH THE FLOW

I tell myself I have too much to lose.
I am fearful to allow you into my world.
I've met them in every shape and form—
Hearts that have been dragged across
rocky terrains and thrown off cliffs
and never found again.
Doubts hinder my feet, and I tiptoe.
You feel my hesitancy and coax me
into the water.
And when I feel the waves caress shoulders
that carry the weight of the land,
I lie back, and against all odds,
try to go with the flow.

SHAKEN, NOT STIRRED

I have sea legs as I navigate me and you.
I am shaken but not stirred,
and you handle me
like the drink you've been needing
all day.

CREATIVE THREADS

You can share your dreams and passions
with others and, even if they see the flames
licking in your eyes, they will not feel the
fire warming them *the way it warms you.*
Try not to take it to heart. Try not to let it
smother your flame. We are all unique, with
different creative threads that appeal to
the passions woven in our souls.

WHAT REMAINS

I sometimes wonder if I'm alone,
or if there are others who feel like me.
We love. And then we experience loss.
But what do we do with all of the love that
still remains?
Do we throw that away, too?

SOMEWHERE ELSE

I never felt like I belonged where I dwelled.
My voice was too high.
My head hung too low.
I was too much for some, and not enough
for most.
I walked with unease, always thinking
I needed to be somewhere else, making
a difference.
Or maybe somewhere else was supposed to
make a difference out of me.
Somewhere else.
Anywhere else.

ULTIMATUM

I let him go
because my heart
gave me an ultimatum.
It refused to keep
on beating
and endure
my grieving.
It made me choose
between him
and living.

IN WAIT OF YOU

Tell me how long
a normal heart can stay frozen
while lying under the full sun.
Now tell me how long
I can stay frozen
while lying
in wait of you.

WE WANT IT ALL

We want the ones who are capable of calming
our souls and exciting our hearts.
The ones who straddle the fence between
masculinity and feminine understanding.
The ones who don't believe there's only one
way, but understand there are different
ways for individual hearts to
find fulfillment.
The ones who inspire us to run, but catch us
if we fall. The ones who aren't expected to
save us, but want to save us.
We want both the hard and the soft.
We want it all.
We want.
We want it all.

ON POINT

I know how it feels to hold pain inside that
is invisible to the outside world.
Transformation does that.
It always takes place within you.
So you ache from morning to night, with
no release.
Feeling your chest rise and fall as it shifts
the weight of the world around.
And no one knows,
because your acting is on point.

VISITING HOME

It is said that all life emanated from the
sea, *so on some level,* it calls to each of our
souls differently. We soak in baths and let
the comfort sink into our bones. We jump in
pools and let our bodies *swim free*
and weightless.
We speed in boats, fish off piers, and cruise
on ships. We gather on shores and stand in
awe at the force of the current.
We are drawn toward a life force that has
the power to call each of us home for a
periodic visit.

I BELIEVE HIM

He has the ability to calm the turbulence
that overwhelms me.
He looks at me and tells me that *everything
will be okay* as he holds my quaking hand.
And even though those words are empty to
souls who are swimming in the abyss
of despair,
I believe him.

TOO LATE

Sometimes it doesn't work out, not because
the passion isn't there, but because fear has
our hearts surrounded by fog.
And if you have encountered storms in the
past, or severe weather, you will generally
wait it out.
But sometimes, when we can finally see
clearly, *it's too late.*

MAIDEN OF THE MOON

A sunrise
is not always
a beautiful sight
to a maiden of the moon.
She is far too fond
of the way she feels
in the moonlight.

THEY NEED ME

I gave myself away
in such a way that
I became indispensable.
They depended on me.
They needed me.
I made them need me.
And it worked for a while.
But that's not the same
as someone loving you
for you.

HONESTY

Surround yourself with truth.
Honest friends will inspire you to have
truthful life experiences.
Don't lie to yourself and tell yourself it's
okay if feelings, conversations, and
relationships are not authentic.
Address the hurt caused by distrustful
behavior before it grows in your heart and
establishes false boundaries.
It's the only way you will insist on leading
an honest life.

DESPITE THE OBSTACLES

If you dare to accept the possibility that happiness is attainable *despite the obstacles* you will face in life, then you *will not* become a victim of circumstances.
You will become a survivor.

RESPONSIBILITY

I let more things go *than I keep* these days.
Owning something requires responsibility.
We must be good caretakers of everything we
possess, and my track record has not always
been upstanding. *Just ask my heart.*

A LIFETIME GRIP

Don't believe the ones who have the
loosest grip.
The ones who do just enough
to keep you waiting.
They know you are the kind
that holds on with arms of steel.
They brush you with
reassurance as light as a feather.
You deserve the one who has
a lifetime grip.

HEART SECRETS

Are you listening to the words your heart
keeps hidden?
Press your ear to the door and learn all of
its secrets.

REMINDING MYSELF

I have to remind myself that if I close up
and collapse into myself, I'm not releasing
the things that *need to go*.
The unwanted guests that treat my nooks
and crannies like vacation homes.
The memories that paint the walls, and the
possessions I hoard that decorate rooms.
I remind myself that others hurt the way
I hurt.
I'm not alone in this world.
Even if I feel like I am.

OFF YOUR FEET

When the salty winds knock you off
your feet,
and there are no hands reaching to pull
you upright,
Kneel while you're low.
Never forget that everything can change for
the better in the blink of an eye.
No situation is final.
We tend to think that every storm is the
last and *this is the big one.*
But it's not. You have to keep yourself in a
positive state. You will get through this.
And *you will* find the strength to
stand again.

MOST VALUABLE

It takes an extreme amount of courage to
open your heart and allow another to
peek inside.
You want to love fully, yet at the same time
you have to keep a measure of love
for yourself.
So instead of using a measuring cup, you
walk a tightrope that is blowing in the wind
and you go back and forth. And one day you
learn how to love someone with everything
you possess.
It takes practice, but you never forget that
self—love is the most valuable possession
you own, *and you do not relinquish it
to anyone.*

OUT OF THE EQUATION

Don't be the one *he misses.*
Be the one he's with
because he could never
handle missing *you.*

LOCK AND KEY

The hardest part about reflection is trying
to figure out *your own place* in the memory.
The way you remember it is seldom the way it
actually happened. Your heart sugarcoats
events and dresses them in finery you could
never afford. And if that doesn't work,
it uses the twentieth filter of your
camera roll.
*So, instead, you hold tight to the dreams
you've never given up on.* The dreams for the
future that you've stored away under lock
and key.
Because you know they would not be alive
and thriving in your heart if there wasn't
a chance.

ON THE HORIZON

I have intercoastal dreams.

You on one side.
Me on the other.
And somehow we overcome
the distance that we have allowed
our personal passions to become.
And somehow we meet on the horizon.

NO RIGHT, NO WRONG

Some hearts aren't meant to hold on forever, but that doesn't make them any less strong. Whether you are burning the ports of the past and moving on, or have set your anchor firmly in the sand—both take acts of God. Remember to do what your heart *and your head* tell you to do.

CHARIOTS OF FIRE

There are some who cannot handle her
essence. Her light is orange red. Her aura
is *raging from exposure.*
Chariots of fire racing down streets you
are afraid to venture.
Cinders dancing across abandoned
storefronts and backstreet meeting rooms.
A scenic lightshow across weary brows.
Hands too hot to touch unless life has
tempered your soul and prepared you for
their warmth.
She is a woman who has finally found her
worth raging within her.

GRATEFUL TO SING

I have been strong for so long that I can
almost forget the weight of fear.
Almost.
My armor still rides up and exposes the
scars where fear chewed its way out of
my flesh.
I can almost forget if I keep my body
covered and my voice muffled.
But forgetting is impossible even when the
fear leaves.
I am so grateful for life that I need to sing.

RAINY SEASON

The rain covers me, and I would like to
think that *I feel it* and *it feels me* and that
our connection is sacred. But I look around,
and I see others whom it lovingly touches.
And I realize that we all have the same
chance to experience life's wonderful
abundance, but we have to choose its impact
on our lives *and its absorption.*
And love, just like rain, is all around us.
But sometimes we do not let ourselves *absorb
or feel it.*
Or accept it.

THE DRESS

I still have the dress, you know. Every once
in a while, I unwrap it, and gaze upon the
material that was going to tell the world
you were mine for eternity.
I clutch it in my hands and with each stroke
I remember the last time I wore it.
It's lovely, and I catch my breath as I take
in the workmanship that went into **309**
perfectly placed pearls from the ocean floor
lining the torso. The intricate lace is the
color of whitecaps and sea foam, and it is
the most beautiful thing I have ever owned
in my life. As I hold it in front of me and
look in the mirror, I'm taken back to the day
we almost said, "I do."
And I pack the gown away, along with
whatever hope I still possess, lest that
leave too.
I'm still not ready to let the dress,
or you, go.

HOARDERS

We file our experiences in compartments
that we have tabbed for our own personal
reasons. We close and lock the cabinet door,
assuming we will need them for another day.
We are like that, you know. Habitual
emotional hoarders.
Even if we keep them in order, there are
drawers full, *and they are overflowing.* What
do we learn from any experience if we don't
take the time to study the file instead of
shelving it? Instead of holding on to the
entire thing, why don't we just keep the
parts we can learn from?
*Letting go doesn't always mean letting go of
love.* Sometimes it's letting go of things
that suffocate your potential for a fruitful
and blooming future.

DRUNK ON YOU

When you offer
all of yourself
to him,
and he decides
to drink it all
in one full gulp,
you will feel consumed
and he will become
drunk *on you.*

SHALLOW DEPTH

I finally move
an inch forward.
My breath becomes loose
and turns to warm milk.
I feel you tug
and my soul gulps.
Shallow.
I breathe shallow breaths.
And I step back
into shallow footsteps,
and into shallow arms,
in the shallow end of love.

BEDTIME STORIES

I wonder if the moon
tells the stars
bedtime stories.
And each twinkle
in the onyx sky
is a sign
that our solar system
is being wooed
with words
that prompt *their dreams.*

IRREPLACEABLE

I keep the bouquets of wilted roses safe
between the pages of his letters that I could
never bear to part with.
Maybe it all didn't end perfectly, but at one
time *he transformed his love into words.*
And some things are irreplaceable.

GIFTS

You can never adequately prepare for the
way life will surprise you.
But if you look at all the twists and turns
as gifts, instead of road blocks, the
universe will lead the way.

THE DREAM

Tell me.
How do you decide whether to chase your
dream or stay still *and wait for it?*

DIG THE ROWS

You spend so much time dreaming.
Hoping.
Praying.
But you must physically dig the rows
of your garden,
and sow the muddy trenches with hearty
seeds that will bring forth dreams
and yield abundance
tomorrow.

FORCE YOUR SOUL TO REST

Don't discount the dark days of your life.
Every bloom has a dormant phase before it
embarks on a new season.
In times of darkness, *force your soul
to rest*.
Your mind and body need to recuperate.
Implement self-care.
Bathe your soul in inspirational bath bombs
and healing salve.
You must build the strength you need
to bend toward the light.

WHAT TOOK YOU SO LONG?

When we met it was an instant, *"Hello. What took you so long?"* I heard the rusty gates swing forth, allowing your entry, and the sound was as familiar as your voice. Sometimes we meet people in our lives whom our souls have known long before, and it is instant relief to be finally found.

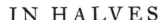

IN HALVES

And even though I'm here,
surrounded by people I see day in and day
out, *my soul is split.*
Half of me resides where love has led it.
It's impossible to live in this world and not
be present with the one who owns
your heart.
I know this, because
part of me is somewhere with him.

LISTEN TO IT

Have you listened to it? The pain that crawls through your veins and scrapes your insides? Listen to it. It's begging you to acknowledge it and learn from it.

I know you've heard this before, *but don't ignore it.* At some point, you may think it's gone and that you're a miraculous survivor because it has become a manageable side effect. *But pain hasn't left.* It isn't through with you yet. It's too comfortable.

It is squatting under a rib and staying out of sight. It's made a home in your neglected heartache and is quite comfortable. Pain is saving its energy so it can conjure up all that doubt in your heart when it sees you on the brink of happiness. It's figuring out the best way to knock you to your knees with an anxiety attack that comes out of nowhere. It's practicing its voice for when you look in the mirror and hear "You're not worthy."

NOT EVERYTHING IS FIXABLE

I can't fix everything.
I look at the shattered pieces of the world.
And *I try*. **I've tried.** I can bandage up
wounds. I can glue pieces. But what is it
about me *that makes my hands long to heal?*
I've had to force myself to accept that I
cannot fix *irreconcilably* broken.
I couldn't even fix our severing.

LIFE HAS POWER

I will sing our soulful journey until my last
breaths are sung from my offspring.
Our story was spun from a ballad of longing
that trespassed over borders erected to
keep us apart.
How can a life deny two hearts the proximity
that merges their beats?
And why do we give life this power?

BE LIKE YOU

I wish I could be more like you.
Gone with the wind and blowing in a
direction that leads you wherever your soul
chooses to fly.
I wish I could let go like you.
Press onward without a backward glance and
leave one life to pursue another.

UNAFRAID

Some souls are *unafraid* to take chances.
They raise their hands and touch stars.
They syphon the universe of every
magical thing it contains.
And they live with passion.
I did this once.
And I found you.

SLOW BURN

It started out slow
and then burned uncontrollably.
Our love was friendship on fire.
It was the kind of bonding that renders
passion *flammable.*
Maybe I'm drawn to the water because
I'm trying to ease the hurt
and douse the flames that continue to burn.

REMAINS OF US

I come to the beach to remember all the good
that *remains of us.*
Maybe it's selfish to discard a life I've
worked so hard at for a few undisturbed
days of relaxation that are permeated by
your memory.
We all heal *in our own fashion,* and at a
pace in time that cannot be understood
by others.
But the therapy I seek and bask in is the
sunshine upon the salty shores *that are
heavy with you.*

I ACCEPT IT

I've learned to look at life with shrewd
vision. It is not *what I think it should be.*
It's not.
I could turn it upside down and point out
all the flaws, *which I have done in the past.*
But no more. I will roll with the punches. I
will get smacked in the face with waves I
never saw coming, and I will build strength
while experiencing the thrashing. Because
that's what a survivor does. *I accept it.*
I accept life, *with discernment.*
And I will thrive *and choose* happiness.

DRAWING A BLANK

Too many mornings I have walked alone *with my thoughts*. My mind always replays the scenarios I have invented to excuse your absence.
But after all this time, my mind is drawing a blank. The ocean has done its duty. It has cleansed me of the last *residue of us*.
My soul is ready to be filled by new memories and is excited to pursue the life of my dreams.

NEVER AGAIN

You'll think about me
every time you're lonely.
But by then you'll know
I'll never be lonely
again.

GOODBYES

The rocks are slippery with ocean tears as
I try to adjust my footing. I hold the bottle
in my hands as the sun kisses the celadon
aqua glass. I've waxed the cork in lover's
red, hoping to keep my prayers safe
and cocooned.
Maybe someone who finds this will know
that, although love is not a choice, *setting
it free is.*
Goodbyes come in all shapes and forms,
and mine will be *received and delivered* by
the salt of the sea.

Acknowledgments

To Kevin, my children, my mom, and my family, who have had to endure my hermit status. Thank you for loving me. *I love you.*

Regina, I will always love you for believing in me and for your gentle nudge.

Ashley, Nicole, and Stephanie. Your unwavering friendship and *belief in me* are the reasons I was able to write this book. I love you.

To Jesus Christ. You are the reason in every season of my life. Thank you for taking me on the pathway that has led me to today.

A big thank-you to my readers. This is for you!

Also by Alfa: